# FACING THE
# DRAGON

## A Motivational Story

### Disclaimer

This book is presented solely for educational purposes. The author and publisher are not offering it as medical, financial, business, or any other type of advice. Every individual is different and the advice and strategies contained herein may not be suitable for your situation.

While best efforts have been used in preparing this book, the author and publisher make no representations or warranties of any kind and assume no liabilities of any kind with respect to the accuracy or completeness of the contents and specifically disclaim any implied warranties of merchantability or fitness of use for a particular purpose.

Neither the author nor the publisher shall be held liable or responsible to any person or entity with respect to any loss or incidental or consequential damages caused, or alleged to have been caused, directly or indirectly, by the information or programs contained herein. No warranty may be created or extended by sales representatives or written sales materials.

This is a work of fiction. Names, characters, businesses, places, events, locales, and incidents are either the products of the author's imagination or used in a fictitious manner. Any resemblance to actual persons, living or dead, or actual events is purely coincidental.

# FACING THE
# DRAGON

## A MOTIVATIONAL STORY

## CARLOS KANO

# INTRODUCTION

What did you want to be when you grew up? An astronaut? An artist? An athlete?

Did you want to change the world?

When we're young, we're told that anything is possible. But as we get older, society starts to send us a different message. Reaching for our dreams is too hard, we're told. And that often seems true. We are told to take careers that are safe, that are common, that we can rely upon to pay the bills.

When we do that, our sense of life purpose often becomes divorced from our career. We have spent too long listening to how society defines us. But that sense of purpose we knew as children still lives inside us.

This book is for those who want a purpose-driven life. Whether your life purpose is to experience all that life has to offer, to be the best parent you can possibly be, or to be the best artist, scientist, stock broker, or athlete - all of these purposes are good and useful, and all of them require a few common elements:

1. Recognition of our purpose.
2. Dedication to realize our purpose.
3. The "habit of excellence" - the full investment in ourselves of achieving our purpose.

You may be a student who's just starting to be told by adults that you must decide what to do after high school. Or you may be an office worker who has spent decades in the corporate world, and knows you're supposed to be doing something more.

There are a million self-help books out there that will coach you in steps that will make your life better if you follow them. But many of us get enough to-do lists in our lives.

In this book, I'd like to do something different. Instead of telling you what to do, I'd like to invite you to take a journey of the heart with me.

I'd like to invite you into a world just like ours, but different in one way. In this world, a person's life purpose is something they can *see*.

May the story of Jonah finding his life purpose be of service to you in finding yours.

# CHAPTER 1

Jonah slammed his locker shut and tried to become invisible. Other teenagers streamed past him, talking and and laughing excitedly. He seemed to be the only kid in school who wasn't either excited about graduation, or cool enough that he could successfully pretend not to care. His best hope right now seemed to be to pray no one noticed him until the ceremony was over.

Today was the prelude - the pep rally, where the teachers and principle would remind the students, *again*, of the excitement that lay ahead of them. They were about to go out into the world as adults, where they would work even harder than they had in high school to become masters of their chosen career or craft.

There was only one problem: Jonah didn't want to.

He'd been through the art classes, and he loved drawing, but he recoiled when the counselors told him they didn't think he'd test well as an artist. He'd been through the business classes, and he loved the idea of building something new, but he couldn't think of what product or service he would sell. He'd been through chemistry class and loved learning how things worked, but when he tried to do equations, the answers never came out right.

So when the others went off to their colleges or trade schools or apprenticeships - what was he going to do?

He started walking, very slowly, in the opposite direction from the other students. He hoped that in the throng, no one would notice him.

It must have worked, because he hadn't taken five steps before someone crashed into him, knocking him over.

"I'm sorry! I'm so sorry," Jonah started, scrambling to pick up the books and pencils that had spilled everywhere. As he stuffed them back into his open bag on the floor, he looked up - and found himself staring at Mike Miller, the class valedictorian.

"Hi, Jonah," he said.

*He knows my name.* "H-hi."

"Are you going to the pep rally?"

"Of course! I'm just - getting something from my locker."

Mike looked uncertain as he watched Jonah. Probably, Jonah thought, because he was so clearly terrified.

"It's okay, you know," Mike said softly, "to be afraid of graduation. It's a big change. Lots of people are scared of it!"

"I - I'm not scared of graduation!" Jonah stuttered. "I just...left something in my locker."

Mike smiled the kind of smile that drove Jonah nuts. It

was the look his mom got sometimes, when she knew she was right about something.

"I'd better get going," Jonah rushed, "if I'm gonna get to my locker before the rally!" Around them, the flow of students had slowed to a trickle. That meant almost everyone was in the auditorium - and if he left now, it was likely no one would notice.

Mike moved on, shaking his head, as Jonah darted for the doors at the end of the hall.

Outside, the air was fresh and the Sun was bright. Jonah took a deep breath. The older students' cars surrounded the high school in neat rows, stretching out across the asphalt of the parking lot.

Jonah didn't have a car yet. And even if he had - he didn't know where to go, or what he'd do when he got there. Would he go home and lie on his bed, staring at the ceiling of the room he'd had since he was nine years old? Or would he go to the local diner, order pancakes, and stare at the wall?

It didn't seem to matter. But it was a beautiful day, with a bright blue sky and birds singing in the trees. So Jonah decided to walk.

He walked beside the little two-lane road toward his house, the occasional car whizzing past him as he walked. To either side of the road, tall evergreen trees reached for the sky. Occasionally, Jonah heard a small squirrel or rabbit rustle in the underbrush beneath them, startled by this unexpected human.

He loved living in the mountains - and that was one of the things that scared him about graduating. His teachers said all the good jobs were in the big cities, that that was where you had to move if you wanted to be a doctor or a programmer or a businessman. His classmates talked excitedly about moving into a glittering skyscraper like the ones they saw on TV, about having an office there high above the city.

Jonah thought the city skylines were pretty, but not as beautiful as a tree. And he couldn't imagine himself among the people in suits, sitting at desks all day and drinking fancy cocktails while they talked business.

In fact, if he was honest, the whole idea of trading stocks or taking people's money repulsed him. It all seemed so... meaningless.

What was wrong with him, that he couldn't be like Mike Miller and the other confident, gorgeous seniors who looked like they belonged in suits with cocktails in their hands? Why couldn't he even *want* that?

The sun was low in the sky by the time his family's little house came into sight. The wooden bungalow sat at the end of a long, winding driveway, surrounded by steep hills. On the sprawling front lawn, his mom grew vegetables - so many of them that his dad had started to joke she was trying to start a farm. Jonah's dad had been raised on a farm, but now he worked as an auto mechanic in town.

Jonah was tired and thirsty, but he didn't want to go home yet. He didn't want to sit in his room, or face his parents at the dinner table when they asked him how school was today.

Instead, he went around the back of the house and snuck up to his bedroom window. The white-painted frame was loose and the window had no screen, so it was easy to lift open from the outside. He climbed in and, very quietly.

The walls of his room were painted sky-blue - his favorite color. A handmade quilt his grandmother had made before she died was spread out on his bed. He got down on the wooden floor and reached under his bed, pulling out a big metal flashlight and a comic book.

Jonah knew the other kids at school considered him "a baby" because he still read comic books by flashlight instead of going to parties and getting drunk. But he was too shy to talk to girls, and he didn't really see why they liked parties anyway.

He cracked open his bedroom door, listening carefully for any sounds in the house. Silence. That meant his dad was probably still at work, and his mom was likely knitting in the parlor on the other end of the house, like she liked to do before dinner.

Perfect. He crept slowly into the kitchen, avoiding the floorboards that squeaked too loudly, and grabbed a can of soda and a bag of potato chips from the kitchen cupboard. Then he took a pen and a piece of paper from a pad on the table, and wrote:

*Gone to Kevin's. Probably going to spend the night. See you tomorrow afternoon.*

*Love, Jonah*

That was another thing he didn't like about the idea of graduation. Jonah didn't want to live in his childhood bedroom, answering to his parents, forever. But the idea of adopting a totally different lifestyle - one his parents wouldn't fit into - didn't appeal to him either. If he stayed out here and became an auto mechanic, other kids would say he was a "loser." But if he went to the city and tried to keep up with the Mike Millers of the world, he was sure that after a few years, his parents wouldn't recognize him.

Looking around the kitchen with its old, creaking cupboards one last time, he scampered out of the front door and down the front steps.

He skirted around his mom's vegetable patch, stepping carefully through the high grass around it, and trekked through the meadow behind the house toward the mountain trail.

The trail was one that hikers used to come from a nearby national park. People from town snuck up there, sometimes, but usually when they wanted to get drunk or party far from the eyes of the adults. Jonah just wanted to be alone.

As he hiked along the dirt trail that skirted the edge of the mountain, the sun sank toward the horizon in the west. He stopped at a little overlook - a spot off the trail, where the trees and brush cleared and you could see over the valley and its town.

From here, a few twinkling lights glittered in the squat buildings of the diner, the auto shop, the school where some sports game was probably happening in the gym. Little cars wove back and forth along the narrow roads, their headlights glowing light fireflies.

But the real majesty was on the horizon: the sun turned orange as it sank, transforming the sky around it into shades of orange and gold.

Jonah sat on the overlook and pulled out his can of soda

and bag of potato chips. There was nothing like a good sunset and a good snack at the same time.

But as he ripped the potato chip bag open, behind him he heard a different sound. It was the sound of footsteps - slow, heavy, and cautious. Unmistakably, the footsteps of a human who had seen Jonah.

Jonah froze. Campers and - well, *everyone* who came up here, were harmless. The empty wilderness was a terrible place to come if you wanted to rob or kidnap someone. But running into people on the trail was so rare - especially *here*, miles from the nearest actual camping ground, at sunset.

Jonah reached into his bag and curled his fingers around the handle of his flashlight, ready to use it as a weapon. He turned cautiously, and saw -

An old man. An old, *smiling* man. The top of the man's head was bald, and the face beneath his bushy white beard looked like it had never frowned. The old man's mild blue eyes rested on Jonah, as he clomped out of the underbrush with heavy farmers' boots.

"You took my favorite sunset spot," the old man observed.

Jonah picked up his bag and scrambled to his feet. "Sorry! I didn't know anyone came up here at night."

"You don't have to apologize. Stay a while. You look like you need it."

Jonah watched the old man uncertainly. Part of him said that being alone with a stranger on a mountain at night was the last thing he wanted to do. But this old man looked like he literally wouldn't hurt a fly.

Cautiously, hand still wrapped around the flashlight in his bag, Jonah sat down near the edge of the overlook.

For a long time, neither he nor the old man said anything. There was no sound except the crunching of Jonah's potato chips, and the hiss as he opened his soda can. Over the city, bright stars appeared in the darkening blue sky.

"So," the old man asked, finally, "you running away from home, or from something else?"

"What?! I'm not running from anything!"

"Sure. You're by yourself, up here in the middle of nowhere, on a school night, just because you wanted to be."

"Maybe I did, okay? I like the mountains."

The man eyed him sidelong. "If you're running away from something," he said, "you came to the right place."

Jonah stopped mid-crunch through a potato chip. "Why's...why's that?" He asked, finally.

The old man crossed his legs and looked out over the city. "Have you ever been on a magical adventure?" he asked.

"That's...a weird change of subject."

"It's no change of subject at all. You're running from something down there, in the ordinary world. It stands to reason what you're looking for is out *here* - in the magical world."

"This *isn't* a magical world."

The man turned to him, his eyes glittering in the darkness. "Isn't it?"

Jonah stood up. "You know, I think I'd better be getting home." He slung his bag over his shoulder. "My parents will get worried soon..."

"Do you really want to go back there?"

Jonah turned away from the old man and started hiking back toward the trail.

"You can go back there," the old man called, "but nothing will have changed. You want things to change, you need to change *yourself*."

Jonah stopped mid-stride. The old man didn't seem crazy - except for the things he was saying. He moved and talked like someone who had led a long, full, happy life. *Definitely* a long life.

Jonah looked back, hesitantly. The old man was standing on the trail at the edge of the clearing, looking like he was just waiting for Jonah to come follow him.

"You can help me change myself?"

"I can't help you. Only *you* can do it. But I can show you how."

"I..." Jonah looked down the trail leading back to his house. Looked back at the old man, and the mountain trail disappearing into the woods.

He turned around, and followed the old man up the mountain. He wasn't sure what he was doing - but he felt like he had nothing to lose.

# CHAPTER 2

Jonah and the old man hiked in companionable silence under the stars. Jonah watched the man out of the corner of his eye as they went. The old man just seemed so sure of himself, and so peaceful. So *happy*. And *he* lived in the middle of nowhere. Maybe that's what Jonah was meant to do.

"Can I ask…where we're going?" Jonah asked finally, as the moon climbed high in the sky.

"Not much further now. It's a place you've never been before. You'll like it."

"But…why are we going there? I mean, what can we do there that we can't do back there?" Jonah jerked his thumb back toward the town.

"Oh you *can* do what must be done back there. But it's harder. It's easier if I show you how it's done out here, in a place where the rules are a little different."

"What rules?"

"Well, where we're going, you can *see* things that are invisible in the ordinary world. Things that you know are there, that you can feel and know to be real, but…you can't see them. People these days aren't always so good about paying attention to things they can't see."

"Like, ghosts and spirits?"

"No, boy. Nothing outside yourself. But there are *parts* of you, you see, that you can't see with your eyes in the ordinary world. Those parts have a lot to offer you. So it's better if we go where they can talk to you in a way you can't ignore."

The man veered off the trail suddenly, plunging into the dark woods. Jonah scrambled for the flashlight in his backpack, and followed him.

They picked their way through thick underbrush, stepping under low-hanging branches and over fallen logs. Jonah got pine needles in his hair, and a dry branch scratched his arm as he ran into it.

The old man made his way ahead with perfect confidence, like he'd come this way a thousand times before. But looking around, Jonah could see no trail or footpath that they were following.

Jonah *felt* it before he *saw* it. The air got cold, as though they were walking near water. There was a sort of hum in the air. Reality, and his perceptions, seemed to *vibrate*.

"Are you sure this is safe?" Jonah asked the old man, and his voice sounded strange and muffled to his own ears. The old man didn't answer him, but he still moved ahead with perfect confidence.

Then Jonah saw the glow. As the old man stepped over a particularly big log, a soft green glow reflected on his skin, as though there were neon lights nearby.

"What are we…"

The old man took another step, and vanished. He was simply gone.

Suddenly alone in the darkness, Jonah froze. He was terrified to move forward, but he wasn't sure he could find his way back on his own.

He didn't understand what had happened to the old man - or if he wanted the same thing to happen to him. But if he did go back now…then what? And the old man had seemed so *happy*.

Jonah took a deep breath and walked forward, using his flashlight to carefully scan the ground.

He stepped over the same log the old man had crossed, and found himself standing in water. It was a shallow marsh - only a few inches deep and crystal clear. Where his flashlight shown at his feet, Jonah could see the brown, dead leaves at the bottom of the pool.

He looked up then, and saw it. In the middle of the shallow pool, an eerie green light shone from the ground, silhouetting the maple, oak, and hickory leaves on top of it.

What in the world was this?

Jonah pushed himself to take another step forward. He put his foot down very gently on the glowing leaves with the green glow underneath them.

Or tried to. Where the ground should have been, his foot instead hit…air?

He understood, now. Taking a deep breath, he steeled himself and -

Jumped. He fell *through* the sheen of water and into open air. He thudded onto -

The softest ground imaginable.

Jonah sat up, testing the spongy surface with his fingers. The ground was covered in something like moss, but it was several inches deep, and it was *violet*.

It was night here, too, but the whole world was illuminated by the light of a huge, full moon and brilliant stars.

Jonah rolled over, sitting on the blue moss in amazement. Around him sprouted a forest like none he'd ever seen.

'Jungle' might have been a better word. The trees had huge palm-like leaves, dark against the stars. This pool - where faint, blue light shone from beneath a thin layer of sand and water - was in the middle of a clearing, with a clear view of the sky above. Jonah couldn't see it, but he was somehow sure from the way the branches of the trees hung low that they were heavy with delicious fruit. The air smelled of flowers.

"Welcome," said a cheery voice next to him, "to the other side of the veil."

The old man was sitting on blue moss a few feet behind Jonah, looking perfectly content. In fact, he looked like he was ready to curl up and go to sleep.

"I...thanks. Where the heck are we?"

The old man chuckled. "I just told you! It isn't anywhere in the world you know, if that's what you're wondering. This is an entirely different world. A *parallel* world. It's a world where you can see what's invisible back home."

"I...great." The old man spoke as though Jonah should understand what that meant, should attach some profound importance to it. But it made about as much sense to Jonah as saying they'd gone to Mars. Less, in fact - Mars was a *place*. This didn't seem to be.

"We...uh...so are we...there?"

"We've come as far as we can tonight," the old man told him, folding his jacket over his head and curling up on the soft moss. "We'd better get a lot of sleep here. You're going to need lots of energy in the morning!"

"The morning - but..." Jonah started to protest that he had school, then realized that he really didn't want to bring that subject up. If going on an adventure with a crazy old man meant getting out of school, so be it.

"Sleep tight!" the old man exclaimed.

Jonah curled up and tucked his bag under his head. He realized that he should have been hungry - he hadn't had dinner - but he was too exhausted to feel it. Surely, the old man had a plan. They would both need breakfast in the morning...

Jonah stared into the darkness of the trees. As he watched, one blue light appeared. It had a soft, mystical quality to it, as though he were seeing it through mist. As he watched, another light appeared, and then another.

Jonah's eyes grew heavy fast, and he fell asleep watching the lights.

❄

Jonah wriggled in his sleep. What was that bright light that wouldn't get out of his eyes? It was like he was sleeping with the windows open -

His head slipped off his bag, and his cheek hit the soft but scratchy moss. His eyes flew open and he found himself staring across a violet meadow, into an alien forest.

Jonah scrambled upright. "I…where…" he looked around for the old man, and found his guide washing his face in the waters of the pool. In the brilliant sunlight, the glow at the bottom was drowned out. Jonah stared at the white sand bottom of the pool, wondering if he'd imagined last night.

But he couldn't have. He was here.

The old man straightened up, drying his face with a towel he'd produced from somewhere. "Well, boy, you'd best get ready. We've a long way to go today."

"We're going…where, exactly?" Now that he was well-rested and thinking clearly, Jonah wasn't going to let the old stranger off without some answers.

"We're going to fight a dragon."

"We…what?"

The old man made a wide, sweeping gesture with his arms. "Does that make less sense than anything you see around you?"

"No…but…*why?*" Fighting a dragon didn't sound like the best idea Jonah had ever heard - or like it would help him feel more at home back in town.

"Dragons," the old man said, "represent our fears. If you can beat a dragon, you can accomplish anything you decide you really want to do."

"And if I can't?" Jonah almost squeaked.

The old man shrugged. "You get burned." He pointed into the waters of the pool. "Do you want to go home? I'll take you home."

"I..." Jonah looked around. Over the forest, birds that looked like tiny dragons themselves were flying. The trees, just as he'd predicted, were heavy with fruit like melons. The air smelled sweet, and the memory of the blue lights in the forest called to him...

"No. But, how badly will I get burned, exactly?"

The old man perked up. "Well, if you do this *right* you won't get burned at all. And if you don't try," he shrugged, "you certainly won't gain anything."

Jonah scrambled to his feet. "Okay, okay. Let's go. Is there food?"

The old man nodded wisely. "Yes. I've been meaning to talk to you about that." Without further explanation, he started trudging for the trees.

"Wait!" Jonah squealed. He half-jogged to keep up. "You've been meaning to talk to me about what?"

"Your diet," the old man said, glancing at him. "If what I saw last night is normal, it can't be helping. How do you expect to slay a dragon if you're living on soda and chips?"

"I don't eat those for *every* meal!" Jonah said indignantly. "Just...for every snack. And where's the harm? It's not like I'm fat, or something."

"How you look isn't the problem." the old man explained. Processed food is not always a great choice for your body. You need to eat food that has the nutrients your body needs to be energetic and healthy. The kind of food your body was made to eat. Too much sugar and salt, though, can slow you down. They won't give you dragon-fighting energy. If anything, they'll make you sluggish."

"I…that's how all the kids eat."

"And do you want to be like all the other kids?"

"…kind of, yeah. Isn't that what we're trying to do here?"

"Heavens no, boy. Anyone can 'be like all the other kids.' What we are looking to accomplish here is something special."

"Well you didn't ask me if I wanted to be *special*. You asked me if I wanted to be different from how I already am."

"And you are special. And you will always *be* special. I can't undo that. What I can do is give you the tools to be special *successfully*. To use your greatest strength instead of feeling inadequate because of it."

"My greatest strength? How can you know what my greatest strength is? You don't even know my name!"

The old man shrugged. "What's in a name? I know *people*. And you, boy, walk a little different. You walk like *me*."

"Like you?" Jonah tried not to be too flattered. After all, he didn't know the old man, either. But…he had decided to follow him just by watching him move, hadn't he?

"Tell me, boy: what do you want from your life? Who do you want to *be*?"

"I…" Jonah's mind dried up, at that. He pictured himself in a suit, sipping cocktails. That didn't feel right at all. He pictured himself as his dad, coming home from the auto shop exhausted each day. That didn't feel right either. He pictured himself as a farmer. The farmer in his mind was old and happy and wise - just like this old man.

"I guess I want to be like you."

"And why is that?"

"Because...well, the other kids all say I should go to the city and get a good job. The teachers say that, too. They're so proud of Mike Miller and Cindy Hutton, the way they dressed up for that career fair and the way they seem to know everything about everything. My parents want me to stay around in town, get a job at one of the local businesses. But the other kids say that only losers do that. But my parents will be unhappy if I move away..."

"All of that is what *other* people want for you. That's not what I asked. What do you want for yourself?"

"Well...that's just it. I don't know." Jonah threw his hands up. "I have absolutely no idea. I guess I want to be like you, because you don't seem to *care* what anybody else thinks."

The old man nodded decisively. "Very good."

"I...what?"

"As long as you base your self-worth and confidence on what other people think of you, you will never be happy. Forward thinkers are rarely popular in their own time, you know. The people who change the world are the ones who aren't happy with it as it is."

That line stopped Jonah in his tracks. The old man kept hiking.

*The ones who aren't happy with the world as it is...*

That was him! He wasn't happy with what he knew of the big city, with its miles of grey concrete, its suits and all the competition among those who lived there. There were no trees, no mountains, and people couldn't be themselves. But people also couldn't be themselves back in town - they were always judging each other, and themselves.

"Wait!" Jonah hollered. They were almost at the tree line now.

The old man took a few more steps and stood beneath a dark palm tree. Its bark, Jonah saw, was the color of an old penny.

As he watched, the old man looked up into its branches, and knocked on that scaly, coppery bark.

A huge fruit like a melon fell from the treetop, and hit the deep, soft moss so hard it bounced like a rubber ball.

Jonah scrambled to collect the fruit. When he picked it up, it was hairy like a coconut, but the size and shape of a watermelon. He brought it to the old man.

"Thank you," the old man said, sitting down on the violet moss with the fruit. He produced a folding knife from his pocket and began to cut around the rind. Inside, the fruit was pale green. The old man sliced off a big chunk and handed it to Jonah.

The fruit was sticky and slimy in Jonah's hands. "This is... what is this?"

"Your first diet lesson. The fruit of the copper-barket trees here is very healthy. Just make sure the trees have copper bark - the blue-barked trees have poisonous fruit!" The old man pointed to a grove of blue-barked trees nearby. "But this is the good stuff. Try it!"

Jonah took a bite. It was sweet and crisp, and almost tasteless. It reminded him of a cross between a cucumber and an apple. "It's...not bad," he said reluctantly.

"Not bad? It's fantastic! There's enough fiber in their to clean out your arteries *and* your gut."

Jonah looked down at his stomach. "Do I need...cleaning out?"

"Everybody does. Our bodies weren't made to eat chips and soda, you know. They were made to eat fruits and vegetables.

"They told us that in health class," Jonah muttered. "They told us a lot of things in health class."

"Well this isn't about making your teachers happy. It's about making *you* happy. You're not going to be able to fight any dragons - or be who you want to be - if all you get is food that makes you sluggish and clogs you up."

"It's not *all* I get - "

The old man held up his hand. "But be honest. You wouldn't eat your fruits or vegetables unless your parents made you, would you?"

"...probably not," Jonah admitted.

"Then that's one of the things we have to change. If you're going to be like me, you've gotta take care of yourself *for yourself*. Not because somebody else told you to."

Jonah regarded the slice of sticky green fruit in his hand. "And this will help with that?"

"Tremendously," the old man said.

Jonah ate until he was full.

Together, he and the old man were only able to eat about half of the fruit. The old man lowered the remains to the ground and said: "There. The fairies will get it."

"Fairies?!"

"You didn't think there'd be fairies? You can see them at night, dancing in the trees. Watch out for them, though.

They can be helpful in moderation, but they're not the best of influences."

"…fairies…" Jonah repeated.

"Come on," the old man said. "If we want to be back here by the end of the week, we should get to the edge of the desert by sundown today."

"Desert?" Jonah asked. But the old man was already walking away, into the dark forest.

# CHAPTER 3

Jonah had expected the magical world to be...well, magical. He had not expected it to be *scary*.

Fairy tales were supposed to be full of beauty and wonder. They weren't supposed to involve *big*, dark beasts slinking between the trees just close enough that Jonah could hear them rustling through the brush, or fairies that looked enchanting - but also somehow sinister as they peered at him from behind tree trunks while he walked.

Or were they? He guessed maybe he should have paid more attention in that Women's Lit class where they'd discussed the *original* versions of Grimm fairy tales.

The old man seemed unbothered by the monsters. Not as though he did not expect them to attack, but as though he had done this before, and he was ready to defend himself. Jonah wished he had the same confidence. And he wished he had a folding knife.

"You must learn to handle your fear of monsters," the old

man said, slowing his pace to walk beside Jonah, "if you want to be able to have adventures."

"I don't feel like my fear is the problem here," Jonah said, glancing anxiously to the side of the trail where *something* massive shifted in the dark.

"It's not the *only* problem," the old man agreed. "But it's the biggest one. If you're attacked by a monster, there are two outcomes: either you win, or you lose. Either way, problem solved! But when you're *afraid* of them, they are your problem all the time. You might go your whole life without being attacked, but if you're afraid of them, they'll be your problem all the time."

"Can you teach me how to defend myself?"

"I can. But if I do, will you promise me something?"

"…what?"

"*Use* what I teach you. Don't let the monsters in the trees keep you off the path you want to walk."

"I mean, I'm walking here already."

"If I left you, would you turn around?"

"Yes! I don't know what I'm doing here."

"Well you're about to." The old man stopped and stepped briefly into the dark underbrush, his knife in one hand, blade-out. He reappeared a moment later with a long, straight stick. A branch, Jonah realized, from one of the trees.

"You will face many obstacles on your life's journey," the old man explained, "and the knowledge exists that will allow you to beat them all. But you must decide to do so - decide to seek that knowledge, instead of simply taking the path of least resistance."

"What's wrong with staying out of the woods?" Jonah asked.

"You're welcome to do that," the old man responded, "if you're content with it. But you won't be. Not you.

"Now, I'm going to show you how to use a quarterstaff…"

※

Jonah spent the morning following the old man through the motions. Wielding the quarterstaff made him feel strangely powerful. He didn't really know much, but somehow just being given *permission* to defend himself made him hit harder. He fended off the old man while he came at him with a stick - clearly going easy on him, but making Jonah feel like he'd really accomplished something at the end.

"Not bad," the old man observed finally. "Now, mark my words, boy - your best ally on any journey is someone who has walked the same path before you. No book or class can teach you as effectively as a mentor can. Though they can certainly be a good starting point."

The old man whirled and gestured to the forest all around him. "There is one thing you must learn before you even start out on a journey like this one. I suppose I should have told you earlier."

"What's that?" Jonah stared into the ominous darkness.

"Nothing worth getting to can be gotten without facing some frightening challenges. But there is one *very important* choice you can make."

"What's that?" Jonah asked.

"Why," the old man turned to him, smiling, "you can choose which monsters to surround yourself with." He walked around the small clearing they stood in, gesturing. "There are many kinds of monsters, you see. People in your life can become monsters if they treat you badly, drain your energy, or try to stop you from following your path. Hobbies can become monsters if they take up so much of your time that you're not making progress toward your final goal. A bad boss or a bad job can hurt your confidence more than they help your career. A financial or educational challenge can be a monster, too.

"Now, boy, if I were attacked by six different monsters at once, what do you think would happen?"

"I don't think it would go well for you."

"Right! But if I could avoid three or four of those monsters, or take a route which had fewer of them on it, I'd have a better chance of success. Don't you agree?"

"Yeah. But…how do you avoid monsters? Or people like bad friends or bad bosses?"

"Well, the solution to some of these monsters is obvious. If a hobby or addiction is stopping you from making progress toward your destination, only you can choose to stop giving the behavior power over you. But many people face a time in their life when they must drop a friend, family member, or boss, because they are making it too difficult for them to fight the battles they need to keep moving forward."

"'Dropping a person'…doesn't sound very nice."

"Oh, but it *is* very nice. It's the kindest thing you can do. For yourself. And you deserve kindness as much as anyone else does. Don't you?"

"It doesn't really feel like that. I've always been taught that it's mean to exclude people."

"Well if you're excluding them for a terrible reason, like their gender, race, or religion, it is. But excluding a person because of their own actions and choices is a different matter. If someone *chooses* to treat you badly, you don't owe them your time. And if they are really in desperate need of companionship - then *they* can always change. Do you see?"

"I guess so." The old man had started walking again, and Jonah trudged after him, kicking the big, black leaves of the alien trees that littered the forest floor. "But what if someone can't help it? Like if they have anxiety, or a disability, or something?"

"Is there a disability that forces people to treat others badly?" The old man asked. "This is the first I'm hearing of it!"

"No but like - there's this girl at school who can be real mean. She yells at people and puts them down. She says it's because she has anxiety and she just can't help it. Then she cries if she doesn't get invited to a party, and everybody feels really bad."

"Putting others down isn't a disease. It's a choice. Or a habit, maybe. An action she has chosen so many times that it's now harder for her to stop than to continue.

"Her anxiety might make it harder to stop. But it's her responsibility to educate herself and change her behavior. She can even ask for *help* stopping, if she wants to. But I'll bet she's never done that, has she?"

"No! She says it isn't possible for her to just be nice all the time."

"It sounds as though she hasn't tried very hard."

"No...I guess not."

"So if she treats you badly, you are not obligated to invite her to anything. And she doesn't get to blame others when her own behavior causes her to be left out. Would you expect her to invite you over, if you yelled at her and put her down all the time?"

"Of course not! I wouldn't expect anyone to want to be around me if I acted like that."

"Then why let others expect you to tolerate such behavior from *them*?"

Jonah thought about that for a long time, staring at the big black leaves beneath his feet.

"What if, like, it's your family?" he finally asked.

The old man glanced, up, but said nothing.

"Like, my parents are great. But my mom's sister treats her kids really badly. She thinks she knows exactly what they should do with their lives, and she gets really mad if they do anything she doesn't like. Which is everything. How do you like...if your mom is one of your 'monsters'...how do you avoid her?"

"Well," the old man said heavily, "that isn't easy. But it is *justified*. Parents are supposed to help their children be success-ful. Parents are suppose to be supportive and guides for their children the best way they can. It sounds like your mother's sister has some unfortunate ideas. Her children are unlikely to perform well in school programs or careers they don't like. When someone has poor judgement, and tries to force it on other people - you don't owe them your obedience. If a person is not helping you succeed, you don't owe them anything."

Jonah thought about that. Privately, he'd been thinking his mom should stop talking to her sister - she didn't treat her siblings well, either. But he kept those thoughts to himself.

After a long time, he broke the silence again. "This…quest, thing. Is it going to help me be a better person?"

The old man blinked owlishly at him. "I should think so. Can I tell you a secret?"

Jonah leaned closer.

"Society often tells you that the way to be a good person is to make others happy. That's true. But society is quite confused about what causes 'happiness.' What do you think makes people happy, Jonah?"

Jonah shrugged. "I don't know. Having a good job and enough money. Having cool stuff, like a nice house or car."

The old man held up one finger. "Aha! But what if I told you that luxuries like comfort and convenience have *nothing to do* with happiness? Or that they may actually be harmful to it?"

"How can comfort and convenience *possibly* make somebody unhappy?"

"By stopping them from taking risks, or relying on each other! Do you know what the two most *important* causes of happiness are, boy?"

"I…it's not either of those?"

"No. The two main causes of happiness are warm, supportive relationships; and, continuing to fill the heart with love and purpose. All this emphasis on comfort and convenience - it's quite misleading. Being *too* comfortable can actually be dangerous to your happiness. What do you think of that?"

Jonah thought about it. "Well, I guess that makes sense. I'm happier *now* than I was yesterday afternoon, even though I'm surrounded by," he looked around anxiously, "a bunch of monsters."

"Precisely!" the old man beamed. "Now, don't go chasing down monsters for their own sake. But there are no shortage of valuable things - and all of them are guarded by challenges. Choose the things you want, and be prepared to fight the monsters you have to fight to get there."

"I...okay. Hey. What valuable thing are *we* headed for?"

"We," the old man said, "are on our way to the most valuable thing of all. But don't worry about what it is now! You won't be able to understand what it is until you see it."

That didn't make a lot of sense. But following the old man so far, Jonah had had the most exciting - maybe the best - day he'd had in years.

He figured he'd keep trusting the old man a little longer.

# CHAPTER 4

Jonah followed the old man down the path strewn with big, dark leaves. In the forest around them, huge things moved unseen, rustling leaves and breaking branches with loud *cracks*. Beautiful but eerie-seeming fairies danced along the side of the trail and peeked out from behind tree trunks, winking at him.

In time, the trees began to thin. Jonah saw bright sky peering through the branches ahead, as the day faded into green twilight.

At the edge of the forest, the trees simply stopped. Ahead stretched endless dunes of sparkling sand, which blew like powdered snow on the breeze.

Jonah stepped up to the old man's side and stared in wonder. The desert was very beautiful, but also strange as the sun - now emerald green with sunset - sank below the sandy horizon.

"Where are we?" Jonah whispered.

"That," the old man said, "is the Desert of Doubt. It is a treacherous place, and difficult to get through. But it is essential to our quest. Nothing worth having can be obtained without crossing this Desert."

Jonah looked from the old man to the horizon, then back again. "Don't you think my parents will be…"

"Time works differently, here. Do not worry about them: worry about yourself."

Jonah thought about what was in his backpack. It didn't seem as though a flashlight would help them much here. He'd eaten all of his chips, and drunk all of his soda. He hadn't thought to fill the empty cans with water at the pool.

But surely, the old man must have a plan. He knew his way through the forest, after all.

The old man was getting down on the ground, stretching out on the soft sand. Above, the supernaturally bright stars had begun to appear, forming a tapestry across the dark sky.

"The Desert of Doubt," he said, "is a difficult place. We should get some rest before we cross it.

Jonah shrugged and followed suit. He folded his bag up into a pillow, lay on his back, and looked up at the stars.

❁

In the morning, Jonah was awakened by a cold wind. He rolled over, moaning, to see the world brightening into dawn. Around him were tiny tracks in the sand - fairy footprints, he realized. As he watched, the wind blew sand to cover the tracks.

Jonah sat up and shivered. He remembered reading in geography class that deserts get cold at night. At least in that way, this desert worked like a real one. For some reason that was comforting.

Near him, the old man was curled up in a ball, sleeping. Jonah considered letting the old man sleep, but this wasn't like back home, where he could read comics or play video games for hours until something happened.

Besides, he was hungry! Jonah extended one foot, and poked the old man with his toe.

The old man stirred and moaned. He batted one hand blindly in Jonah's direction.

"Hey..." Jonah tried cautiously. Then, more assertively: "Hey! We're on the edge of a desert, and we haven't eaten in a while!" He poked the old man again.

Finally, the old man rolled over and blinked blearily at Jonah. "Oh. I'd forgotten I wasn't alone this time."

Jonah decided not to ask what that meant. He waited, fidgeting, while the old man took his sweet time stretching and blinking up at the brightening emerald sky.

"So, we need more of that fruit, right?" Jonah prodded. He would have gotten the fruit himself, but he was too scared: he was afraid he'd do it wrong, and poison both of them.

The old man finally rolled into a sitting position. "Yes," he grunted. "We do need more of that fruit. But you must learn to find it for yourself. You can't always rely on me to find it for you - if you don't learn how to do what I do for yourself, you won't be able choose your own path the way I do."

Jonah got to his feet. "I'd like to learn..." he hesitated. "But I'm afraid I'll mess up. It could be really bad if I mess up, right?"

"Yes. Trying something new always carries risks. But the faster you learn, the more independent you will be. That's why

I say: watch one, do one, then you're done. You've watched me pick the fruit once - now I'll watch *you* and help you if you mess up. Once I've watched you get it right, you know you can do it on your own next time."

Jonah nodded. He turned toward the forest, squinting up at the tree tops.

They looked the same as the trees near the pool - tall palm trees with huge, black leaves. Beneath the leaves of one tree he saw a cluster of something green - something that looked kind of like a watermelon.

Jonah pointed: "Is that the right kind of tree?" he asked.

"Not quite," the old man said. "Do you see the bark - the blue color of it? Their fruit isn't good for you. You want the trees with copper-colored bark. They're the ones whose fruit is good to eat." The old man pointed to a different tree, next to the blue-barked one.

Jonah approached the tree cautiously. He ran his fingers across the scaly, shiny bark. It was dry, and flaked away under his hands. He knocked on the tree trunk timidly.

Nothing happened.

"Harder than that." the old man said, trundling up beside Jonah. "You can't be timid if you want to get anything done in this world."

Encouraged, Jonah knocked harder, pounding his fist against the tree.

The tree shuddered. But no fruit appeared.

"Are you thinking about what you're asking for?"

"What?"

"Just doing what you saw someone else do may not work. When you're watching me do something, you might not be able to see everything that makes the process work. You have to keep your goal in mind. Know what you want, and why you want it. Ask yourself: what is the next step I need to take to get there. If what you saw someone else do isn't working, ask yourself: why? 'Why' is the key that unlocks every door. If you don't stop asking why something is or isn't working, you'll eventually find the answer."

"Why...why isn't this working?" Jonah murmured. "What do I want, and why? Well, I want fruit, so we don't starve."

The old man looked at him sternly. "A negative is not a very compelling reason. Don't say 'so nothing bad happens.' Think of what positive things the fruit will *give* you. That's much more convincing."

"I mean - I want fruit, so we can be healthy and strong. And you knocked - but that's not working for me. You knocked - I guess it looked like you were *asking* the tree for fruit. So..." Jonah looked up. "Please, tree. Can I have some fruit, so we can be healthy and strong?"

Two large, green fruits dropped down from the branches, thudding loudly into the windblown sand at the base of the trees.

"Excellent work, Jonah!" the old man enthused. He hurried up to one of the fruits and began cutting into it.

As the old man worked, Jonah looked out across the desert warily. In the bright noon sun, the sand had turned a warm, reddish-gold color. It looked like something out of a travel magazine under the violet sky. In fact, it looked warm and inviting - the sand made Jonah think of a day at the beach.

But...there was no water in sight. He remembered reading in travel magazines, about travelers getting lost in the Sahara Desert and never coming out again.

"Can you remind me," he asked, as the old man handed him a big slab of sticky green fruit, "why we have to go through this desert again?"

"Everything worth having," the old man said, "is on the other side of the Desert of Doubt. It is a difficult, painful place - but you know what they say. No pain, no gain." The old man frowned a little. "Proverbs didn't have to rhyme, in my day."

Despite himself, Jonah laughed. "So we're trying to gain... what, exactly?"

"In your case? The confidence you need to be who you are. You are someone who isn't satisfied with things as they are. That means you're made to make them better. But that isn't easy work. Lots of people will suggest that there's something wrong with *you* - not with the systems you see problems with. So you need to have tremendous courage and confidence to be able to stand up to them, and show them that your way is better."

"I'm not sure I *have* a 'way.' I don't feel like I know how to solve any of the things that bother me."

"The first step," the old man counseled, "is knowing what *does* bother you. And paying attention to that. If it bothers you, does it also bother other people? Do they seem unhappy?"

"Not really," Jonah said.

"You might be surprised. Tell me, Jonah, do you feel obligated to be happy? Do you feel like you're *supposed* to be happy, or you'll be letting other people down?"

"I…kind of, yeah."

"Well how do you know the others don't also feel that way? How do you know they aren't just pretending nothing's wrong?"

Jonah thought of Mike and Cindy, and pondered. "I… shouldn't really assume they're unhappy, should I?"

"Don't assume it. But pay attention to what makes you unhappy. Think about how to fix the system, so it works better for everyone. That, I think, is your gift."

Jonah smiled. It felt good. He realized he couldn't remember the last time he'd smiled this wide. No one had ever told him he was gifted before.

"Well," the old man was wiping his fruit-sticky hands on his pants. "We'd better get moving if we want to get to the Garden of Delight by next week."

"By next…week?!" Jonah screeched, scampering after the old man.

"You didn't think something called the 'Desert of Doubt' would be quick and easy, did you?"

"I…no. But, next *week*? My parents…my school…"

"I told you," the old man reassured him, "time works differently here. Don't worry about them. Just worry about yourself."

"I *am* worried about myself now!"

The old man just smiled, and waded through the golden sand.

# CHAPTER 5

In time, Jonah came to appreciate the silence of the desert. There were no birds or beasts or fairies. The old man didn't speak. There were only his own thoughts, which seemed amplified, as though they echoed off the desert dunes.

At first, that was actually pleasant. He'd always gone to places like his bedroom or the forest to be alone with his own thoughts. Sometimes, it felt like his mind didn't work like other people's - other people's minds seemed to be so noisy, and so interested in things he just didn't care about. It was nice to just let his thoughts be, and let them get quiet sometimes.

But sometimes, his own thoughts *weren't* so pleasant.

*You're just not good at anything*, whispered a malicious voice on the wind. Jonah recognized it as his own. *That's why you have to do all this weird stuff to make you feel special - because you're* not.

Jonah glanced at the old man. The old man didn't seem to hear the voice.

*And now you're walking into a desert after a crazy old man?*

*You're going to get yourself killed. You should just go home and try to be happy with the first job you can get. You'll never be really happy with anything.*

Jonah gulped. This wasn't the first time he'd heard these voices - but here they seemed louder than ever before. With nothing soothing or distracting in sight, they seemed to come from everywhere.

*Loser.*

*You can't help anybody.*

*No one wants your kind of help.*

After a while, the old man glanced at him. "Do you hear voices?" he asked Jonah.

"Yes! Can you hear them too?" Relief flooded Jonah. He wasn't just going crazy. But with the relief came shame. Had the old man heard everything the voices had said?

"I hear different voices," the old man said softly. "We each have our own voices of doubt - things our society tells us to try to keep us in line. Most people don't like change at first, you see. After they've seen how much better things can be, they'll warm up to it. But if a person can convince themselves they're happy with the way things are, they will resist change. So we are rarely taught to trust our instincts. Instead, we're taught that the system cannot be improved."

"What...system?" Jonah asked.

"Just the way people do things. Don't get me wrong - sometimes the system works very well. It has been getting better for many hundreds of years. But it can always use improvement. People like you and me, who don't quite fit into the way things are currently done, are meant to help with that."

"Are you…unhappy? You seem so *happy*."

"I'm happy now. I wasn't always. When I was your age, I knew I wasn't satisfied just making a lot of money. I did for a while, you know. Make a lot of money. But - you know how it is. There's a lot more to life than money. But there weren't a lot of people around me who understood that, who felt that discontentment keenly enough to act on it."

"So what did you do?"

"I left, eventually. I left my hometown and my job, and I made my own way. It was very difficult - like this." The old man glanced overhead. Jonah realized then that the Sun had become very hot. He was sweating intensely, and he longed for the comforting shade of the familiar forest. "But I learned so much. And when I came back to my hometown, to my old colleagues, I was able to share so much of what I'd learned with them. Just like I'm sharing it with you."

Jonah was silent for a long time. Part of him tried to imagine what the old man's voices could possibly have been saying to him - it was difficult to imagine someone like that having and doubts at all! But another part of him just wanted the trek to be over.

Why did the Desert of Doubt have to take so *long* to get through?

By midday, Jonah had to stop and sit down. The Sun was high overhead, and Jonah was sure he was getting terribly sunburned. He wished he'd thought to bring sunscreen.

As Jonah plunked himself down on the hot sand, the old man stopped obligingly to sit with him. The old man opened his bag, took out a bottle of water, and began to chug it.

Jonah's mouth was dry. "We...um, when do we get to water?"

The old man blinked at him. "It's...it's a desert. You didn't bring any water with you?"

"I didn't think..."

The old man shoved his half-full bottle at Jonah. "Well, that is lesson #1. You must cross the Desert of Doubt to get to your destination - but you'd better bring enough provisions to make the trip! You don't need a big tent or a bunch of fancy camping gear - but you certainly need water!"

Jonah took the bottle, but he hesitated for a moment.

"Drink it. I know what I'm doing."

Jonah took a deep, life-giving gulp.

"Lesson #1," the old man said again. "When you embark on a journey across the Desert of Doubt - on any journey - always bring what you need to survive. Getting to your destination may require going off the beaten path. You may need to leave behind rivers, lakes, and convenience stores. To make sure you can make the trip successfully, always make sure you have enough to cover the basics.

"And," he continued, "it *is* the basics that will keep you alive. Like right now - you just need water. If you try to bring a bunch of fancy stuff with you, you won't be able to carry as much water."

Jonah drained the last drop from the water bottle and looked up at the old man. "Thanks," he said. "I'll remember that next time."

❈

On the morning of the second day in the Desert, Jonah knew they were in trouble.

The two of them together had drained the old man's water stores the night before. Out here, there was not even the sticky juice of the forest's green fruits to quench their thirst. Jonah found himself longing for the fruit, while the ideas of potato chips and soda now repulsed him.

"I think," the old man said, licking his cracked lips as he stretched, "that we had better split up."

Jonah felt himself go cold.

"I...what?"

"Sometimes you can find things by yourself that you can't find as part of a group. We're obviously not finding what we need together - so perhaps we will find it separately."

"But how will we find *each* other if...?"

The old man looked at him mildly. "Do you think we can go back the way we came?"

No. That felt completely impossible to Jonah's dry mouth and rubbery legs. They couldn't get back to the forest from here. So they would *have* to find something to sustain them in the desert.

Jonah was never going to take water - or anything else - for granted again.

"I'll go this way," the old man called over his shoulder. He was already walking away, toward where the last of the night's stars still shone in the dark green sky.

Jonah turned toward the emerald sunrise. Part of him wished the old man had chosen the other direction. After yesterday's blistering heat, he was not eager to walk *toward* the Sun.

But he had no choice. So he started forward, putting one foot in front of the other in the lime-green light of dawn.

As the morning brightened, he couldn't look up to see what was on the horizon. More than that, he was afraid to. He couldn't imagine the path ahead holding anything but more and more sand dunes - all of them echoing his doubts back at him.

His legs ached. His skin burned. His head pounded. The desert baked around him.

He tried to swallow the dust grains that he breathed in with the hot desert air, but his throat stuck to itself when he tried. Everything within him cried out for water, but there was no water to be found.

As Jonah struggled up one particularly tall dune, he gave up and fell to his knees. He couldn't do this anymore.

If he had had tears to shed, he thought, he would have been crying. He was going to die from lack of water, and it was going to be his fault for lack of preparation. He would have done anything for simple water, something he had always taken for granted -

But then, a new light invaded his vision.

He sat up, squinting into it.

The blinding white light seemed to come from nowhere. It was as though the Sun had come down to Earth right beside him. But instead of feeling blinding hot, this light felt...cool. Soothing. Like water.

Inside of it, a human figure stood. He couldn't see its face, or even tell if it was a man or a woman - it was only a beautiful silhouette, its outlines blurred by the intensity of the light.

*Jonah.* It was a voice in his head, like the voices of his own doubts. But this one was very different. It was gentle. Loving.

*"What do you need, Jonah?"*

*"Water!"* He couldn't speak, so he thought it, pleading.

*"You shall have it. But you cannot always be this lucky. I will not always be able to protect you."*

*"I'll never forget to pack water again,* Jonah promised desperately. *And I'll never take it for granted. And I'll never try to cross a desert..."*

*"Which would you rather have?"* the entity - Jonah decided to call it an 'angel' - asked. *"Comfort - or freedom?"*

Jonah squinted harder. This seemed the wrong time to ask that particular question.

*"You will soon learn,"* the angel said, *"that each comes at the cost of the other. And you will soon learn which makes you happier."*

Jonah blinked.

*"You can travel further if you forego comfort. If you choose to carry water instead of luxuries."*

*"There is no growth in comfort."*

"Okay!" Jonah croaked aloud. "I get it. I just - can I have some water, please?"

*"Yes. Do you know why?"*

"Because I'm dying!" Jonah cried out.

*"Because life is a gift. You were chosen to be here, to come to*

*this place. Therefore, share your gift with others. Teach what you have learned. Pay forward what you have received. And always be grateful for the gift of life. It is the most precious gift there is."*

And with that Jonah was sliding down the far side of the sand dune, kicking up hot, golden grains as he tumbled into -

Water! Cold, clear, sweet water! He simply flailed around in it for long moments, letting it soak into his clothes and skin. Then, he began to gulp.

It was the sweetest thing he had ever tasted.

Water - something so simple he'd always thought of it as 'boring' - was the only thing that mattered in that very moment.

How could he have ever taken water for granted, back in his old life? In that moment water fulfilled his every need! Water was joy, happiness, gratitude, bliss, satisfaction.

Water - something he'd so often taken for granted - gave him *life*.

# CHAPTER 6

The oasis Jonah had stumbled into was complete heaven. It even included a copse of the copper-barked trees, their big, black leaves providing merciful shade. He curled up under them, too tired to summon one of the big green fruits from their branches.

When he awoke, night was falling. The old man sat beside him. Jonah was somehow not surprised.

"How much longer?" he whispered, through cracked and parched lips.

"My guess is we're about halfway through now," the old man said softly. Jonah noticed that he was sunburned too, and a little solemn. But he didn't seem troubled, exactly. Just thoughtful.

"But," the old man amended, "we can rest for as long as you need."

Jonah slept for a long time. He wasn't sure how long - he was too tired to care. The old man had hollowed out half of a coconut-melon shell and filled it with water for him. Every time Jonah woke up, he drank from the melon shell and ate more fruit.

Once in his dream, he thought he saw a human figure, silhouetted against a brilliant white light. He tried to run toward it, to thank it, but it vanished behind some unseen door in his mind. He looked frantically for the door, but just when he found it -

He woke up.

He was lying on his side, staring out over the lake of cool, blue water. Beyond it, it was bright day over the desert. Jonah felt fear, looking at that desert. But he also felt strangely energized. He had not come all this way for nothing.

"Come on," Jonah said, hauling himself up into a sitting position. The old man lay nearby, his arms folded behind his head and his eyes closed as he leaned against a coppery tree trunk.

At the sound of Jonah's voice, the old man popped one eye open, surprised. "Come on where?" he asked.

Jonah got to his feet. His muscles were still sore, but in a good way, like after a particularly hard day in gym class. "We've got to get to the - what did you call it - the Garden of Delight. That sounds like a pretty great place."

The old man raised an eyebrow. "In a way."

Jonah didn't have the patience right now to ask what he meant by that. He stumbled down to the edge of the oasis pool, filled the fruit shell with water, and drank as much of it as he could.

"Careful now!" the old man cautioned. "There's always such a thing as too *much* of a good thing. Even of water."

Jonah slowed down. "You fill your bottles up?"

"Of course."

"And you said it's only one more day?"

"Yes. We should be fine."

Jonah considered that. "Are you sure?"

The old man grinned. "Now," he said, "you're thinking like an adventurer. Here. I'll give you two of my bottles to you can keep track of your own water."

Jonah took the bottles and weighed them, making sure they were as full as possible before putting them into his pack. He was never going to be caught without the essentials again.

"Okay," he said finally. "Let's go."

✳

Jonah's doubts still rang out across the empty dunes - but they seemed to have lost their power over him. Every time one told him *you're not good enough* or *this is a stupid idea,* he remembered the angel's soothing light, and the sweet taste of water after almost dying of thirst.

After being lost in the desert, he could not imagine ever complaining again about being unable to afford the latest video game, or have a fancy new car like Mike Miller. In fact, he felt luckier than Mike. He had experienced things Mike hadn't.

Jonah led the way in the direction the old man pointed, hiking determinedly into the red-gold dunes. He couldn't see it yet, but according to his mentor, the Garden of Delight would be within sight by nightfall.

Jonah rationed his water carefully and made sure to choose the best path between dunes as they marched onward. He'd become something of an expert at dunes by now, he thought - but only by braving so many of them. He wound between them, finding the paths with the fewest obstacles, rationing his water until the sky began to darken into sunset.

Then, as the first stars came out, he saw it.

He had expected to see trees with tall, black leaves rising against the emerald sky. But instead, cutting neatly through the desert was a tall, white wall.

Jonah stopped in his tracks. "What's that?" he asked.

"Those," the old man puffed, hiking up beside him, "are the gates to the Garden of Delight. Or at least, that is." He pointed to a fleck Jonah hadn't seen - it looked like nothing more than a dark spot in the endless wall from here, but Jonah trusted what the old man said.

"Now, Jonah...we don't *have* to go through the Garden of Delight." The old man looked at him anxiously.

Jonah stared. "What do you mean? You took me through the Desert of Doubt where I almost died of thirst, but you don't want to take me into something called the 'Garden of Delight?'"

"Well," the old man hesitated. "The Garden of Delight is the shortest way to your destination. Technically. But it has a way of...slowing people down. You'll enjoy yourself, but it may take you longer to go *through* the garden than around it."

"And what's on the other side of it?" Jonah asked.

The old man winced. "More desert."

"Then we're going through the Garden. I need a break from all this."

"Alright. As you wish."

The stars were coming out above, but Jonah insisted in hiking until he and the old man were just outside the gates of the Garden of Delight. The gates were two stories high, and made of metal that shone brightly under the light of the enormous moon. The metal of the gates curved and looped in graceful arcs, and Jonah imagined his mother wearing something like them as a pendant around her neck.

Jonah's body was aching and weary from the long days' hike, but when they stood outside the gates, he was satisfied. This way he knew that as soon as they woke up tomorrow, they walk through those gates and have some respite from the Desert of Doubt.

He plunked himself down on the sand, happy and ready to fall into an exhausted sleep.

"So," he asked the old man, wearily, staring at the gates as he curled up, "what's inside?"

"Many pleasant things," the old man said, but his voice was grim.

"You sound almost afraid of it."

"It is a dangerous place."

Jonah was too tired to ask more, so he fell asleep and dreamt of a beautiful garden, where the rivers ran with water of majestic light blue, with hints of yellow and purple.

❃

Jonah awoke in the morning under the blinding light of the desert Sun. Tired from yesterday's hike, he'd slept straight through the dawn. He opened his eyes to stare across the windswept dunes - across all that nothingness. Then he rolled over lazily to talk to the old man.

"So how do we - "

Jonah stopped dead. The old man was nowhere in sight. All around him was empty sand. The wind had erased and tracks the old man might have made as he left. Jonah was alone.

In front of him, the enormous gates to the Garden of Delight were open. In the sunlight, he could see that they were pure gold.

He got to his feet hesitantly, slipping on the loose sand. His pack was light as he hefted it - he'd drunk all his water. The old man must have gone in ahead of him, he thought. That was odd. The old man hadn't seemed to want to go in at all last night.

Jonah waded through the hot sand toward the gates. He stopped in front of them for a moment, trembling. Then he stepped inside.

The cool, moist air hit him like a soothing balm. He took a deep, luxurious breath. The air here smelled sweet - like fruit and grass and flowers. All around him, dark vegetation unwound. The trees rose so high and thick, their canopies so dense that they blotted out the sky.

But Jonah could still see - vines with fruits that glowed brightly with neon blues and pinks and violets climbed the trees. Little fairies flitted about, and he caught small titters of laughter from them as they drifted on the cool, sweet air above his head.

Jonah smiled, feeling giddy. This was more like it!

There was only one problem. He was starving, and he didn't know what was good to eat.

He stepped further into the forest, leaving the golden gates and the desert sunlight behind him. Around him, fairies tittered excitedly.

"Hey! Excuse me, do you know what I can eat around here?"

The tiny people only giggled and darted deeper into the forest, as though beckoning him to follow.

Jonah walked slowly and carefully, looking for copper-barked trees on either side of him. But in the glowing of the globes, all the trees seemed to have blue bark. Bushes heavy with shining berries surrounded him on both sides, their leaves snagging his pants as he walked. But he looked at them with hesitation. The old man had said this place was dangerous, and he hadn't explained what the dangers *were*.

"Hello?" Jonah called loudly. The thick leaves and trees around him seemed to absorb the sound of his voice. "Hellooo!?"

He was really beginning to panic. He was lost in a strange land, with no one to guide him. He knew he'd never find his way back across the desert alone.

"Come with us," a fairy whispered sweetly in his ear. He shuddered at the sound of her voice. The tiny woman fluttered delicately to land on his shoulder.

"I...why?"

"We love to meet new people! Come with us, and we'll show you where the best berries grow!"

"I have a friend - an old man. Have you seen him? Did he come this way?"

"I haven't seen him. Sorry. But you look so *hungry* and *tired*. Come with me, and I'll show you the best place to sleep!"

Jonah had started out feeling suspicious of the little woman, but the more she talked, the more pleasant her voice became. The thought of sleeping on a soft bed of moss did sound *heavenly*, and the thought of sweet berries on his tongue -

It wasn't like the old man was around to tell him what was safe, anyway. This fairy would just have to do. He followed her deeper into the darkness.

More fairies swarmed around him as he walked, whispering flattering things to him as he went.

"Did you come here all by yourself?"

"You're so brave!"

"And *strong*. It isn't easy to cross the Desert!"

"We're so glad you have found us! We were beginning to get lonely."

It was strange to have these tiny people be so nice to him. Jonah tried to remember the last time he'd gotten this much attention from a girl - any girl!

He let the swarm of fairies guide him, not really paying attention to where he was going until he took a step - and his foot splashed into cool water!

Jonah jumped, startled, and backed up. When he looked

down, he saw that the water itself was glowing with a faint blue hue. He blinked at it, staring.

"This is the *best* water," one of the fairies enthused, flying in a circle around him. "We picked it out just for you!"

"I…thank you?"

Jonah was hesitant to drink anything that glowed, but he also didn't have very much choice. He took one of the empty water bottles from his bag and knelt to fill it the stream. When the bottle was full, he raised it up to examine it. The water in the bottle glowed so brightly that he could have used it as a lantern! But it looked clean and pure, other than the strange light it emitted.

Jonah took a cautious sip - and nearly gagged! This water tasted like soda. He rolled it around in his mouth for a while. Once, he probably would have found this delicious. But after drinking only water and eating the vegetable-fruits of the coppery trees for the last few days, the sweetness was almost too much to bear.

He took another tentative sip. It felt as though it would be rude to ask the fairies for *different* water, when they were being so kind to him.

He settled down on the bank of the glowing stream, nestling into the soft leaves and moss below him. As he took another cautious sip of water, a small parade of fairies materialized in front of him. "Try these!"

Each of the fairies was carrying a small fruit or leaf. Each of the plant parts glowed faintly in surrounding darkness.

"This one tastes like peanut butter," one fairy exclaimed, holding a golden-glowing berry bigger than her head. Another held out a leave that was speckled with crimson-glowing sparks. "Try this! Try this!"

Jonah blinked. He *was* very hungry. He took the leaf and bit into it tentatively. It crunched between his teeth like a potato chip!

As soon as he started to eat, the fairies swarmed around frantically, bringing more bits of sweet, salty, and crunchy foods for him to eat.

Jonah laid back in the soft leaves and sighed. This really *was* more like it.

# CHAPTER 7

Jonah wasn't sure how much time had passed when he awoke. In fact, he didn't remember falling asleep. He *should* have been well-rested, having slept well in the desert - was it just the previous night? Or had he been here for several days?

There seemed no reason to move from where he was, lying beside the stream, laughing and playing with the fairies. They always kept him supplied with sweet and salty snacks - and they'd taken to telling him stories.

"Tell me more about the hero and the princess," Jonah asked one little blue woman - a particular friend of his - dreamily.

"Okay! Well the hero was getting ready to face the dragon. But there was a problem. An evil wizard knew that the hero was too strong to be defeated, so he tried to tempt him off of the true path instead..."

Jonah lay back in the leaf litter, and felt himself slipping back into sleep again.

As he slept, he dreamed.

He stood in the empty hallway of his parents' house, with its creaking wooden floors and ancient wallpaper. The place seemed *so* quiet and empty, without any fairies fluttering on the breeze and chattering at him.

He walked through the front hall into the kitchen, the floorboards creaking under him as he did so. He thought about his bedroom - that little square room where he escaped from the world, hiding comic books and tasty snacks under his bed. He tried to remember the last time his parents had paid much attention to him - his mom usually only asked him how school was going and to help with the chores, and his dad arrived home so tired at night that he barely had time to talk.

In his dream, Jonah was getting ready for school. He knew he'd go back to a school full of happy, popular people who seemed to know something he didn't - and other unhappy people who hid, somewhat ashamed, around corners and in the back of the lunch room. He knew he'd try not to be seen talking to *those* people, because they all knew the truth - that there was something wrong with them. Just like there was something wrong with him. He was not made for this world.

In his dream he hefted a bag on his shoulder - a bag filled with pointless books, leading to careers he had no passion for. Careers that required hard work and gave very little pleasure. Why do any of that when he could stay *here...*

In his dream, his mother stepped out from behind the kitchen door. "Jonah?"

"Jonah?"

"*Jonah!*"

He woke with a start to find the old man kneeling over

him, shaking him. The man offered him a slab of green fruit, and barked: "Hurry! We've got to get out of here!"

"Wha? Why?"

"I'll explain later. Just follow me!" The old man half-dragged him to his feet, and dragged him, splashing, across the glowing river.

"Hey! What are you doing? I was - resting - " Jonah protested with his mouth, but his legs ran alongside the old man, who seemed to be trying to outrun the fairy swarm.

"Jonah, wait!" they called. "Don't leave us! We've been so lonely!"

"Why are you lonely when you have each other?" the old man called behind them. "You must not be very good company!"

Jonah hadn't thought about it that way.

They stumbled through the dark forest, glowing fruit making the whole world seem surreal. It was impossible to tell where they were or what time it was, Jonah realized, without the ability to see the Sun.

"How long…" he managed.

"Five days," the old man grunted. "It took me that long to find another oasis and come back for you."

"Come back…?"

"This always happens. New heroes get stuck in here. It's so easy, with all the flattery - and the food here makes you sluggish. Remember what I said about too much salt and sugar?"

Jonah stopped in his tracks then, forcefully. The old man kept going for a few more steps, then stopped to stare.

"Hold on," Jonah said. "What if…what if I *want* to stay?"

"You don't really want that, Jonah. Nothing here is good for you. They've just gotten you addicted."

"But what if - it *is* good for me? I mean why does anyone do anything? To have a nice car and a nice job, right? To have good food and a comfortable bed, and friends who want to be around you?"

The old man stared at him. "Is that why you do things, Jonah?"

Jonah had to think about that.

The image of success he'd always been shown had been just that. The smart, hard-working people who made the right choices were charming, with many people praising them and clamoring for their company. They had nice houses and nice cars - not a forest full of fairies, but Jonah imagined the point of those things was pleasure and comfort. And those successful, hard-working people seemed to enjoy everything they did. Why not just stay somewhere where everything was enjoyable?

"I can't make this choice for you, Jonah," the old man said slowly. "If you ask me to leave you here, I will. But you'll never leave. You'll never see your parents again, or have any more adventures."

Jonah paused at that. "What good would any of those things do?"

"Jonah, those things are *real*. They have meaning. If you get out of here, you can learn. You can grow. You can help others. If you stay - they'll only tell you what you want to hear. Whether it's true or not."

*You can help others.*

*'Life is a gift to be shared. You were brought here for a reason.'*

The angel's voice rang in Jonah's head. He remembered the sweet salvation of the water, the vast dryness of the desert.

"Can I...think about it?"

The old man peered into the darkness behind Jonah. "You won't have long to think." Jonah followed his gaze, and saw a small swarm of fairies approaching in the darkness.

Jonah was moving before he realized it. He ran through the Garden, dead leaves crunching under good and sharp of berry bushes tearing at his clothes.

He knew the old man was right - if he let the fairies get to him again, they'd take his choices from him. He would *think* he'd chosen to stay, that he'd made the choice because life here felt good.

But the truth was, there was no 'choice' involved. It wasn't that he wanted to stay here. It was that the fairies had bombarded him with so much pleasure, compared to the outside world, that he was afraid to leave them and go back to the old world. The places he'd loved and the adventures he'd had just days ago now seemed so drab and empty they felt *scary*. He was afraid to be anywhere but here.

That wasn't a choice. It was a prison.

Jonah ran blindly, realizing he had no idea what he was going. He'd left the old man behind because he was afraid to stop. The old man was stronger than him - he was sure the old man could handle the fairies. Jonah couldn't see them again.

Jonah kept running. If he ran in a straight line long enough, he reasoned, he would eventually *have* to hit a garden wall. And once he found the wall, if he followed it long enough, he would eventually have to come to a gate.

He ran until his legs were sore and tired, and he was flushed and gasping for breath. He ran until his legs almost gave out.

Finally, he collapsed onto the leaf litter in the darkness, surrounded by the glowing fruit. He had at least outrun the fairies.

*Jonah.*

He froze. He recognized that voice. Or at least - no, it wasn't the *same* as the angel's voice. But it sounded similar. Felt similar, in his mind.

He sat up cautiously. The clearing around him was still dark - no blinding angel to light it up. But when he looked around him -

Suddenly, there *was* light. It was as though he'd been transported. White radiance filled his vision, as though pouring out from some door to another realm. In its center, a human silhouette.

*Jonah. Why do you fear this place?*

"Because - because I could get stuck," he said aloud. "I could end up not - giving back. Sharing the gift of life. Paying forward, and all that." He stammered, hoping this was the right answer.

The angel seemed to stir, the light around it swirling like the water of a river. *I am not looking for the 'right' answer, Jonah. I am looking for* your *answer.*

"I…I don't want to stay because I don't want to be trapped. Not even by comfort and luxury. I want to be free to…free to go wherever. Wherever I want."

*And where do you want to go, Jonah?*

It seemed like a question he should know the answer to. It seemed like everybody should know *where* they wanted to go, if they knew *that* they wanted to go. But he didn't. "I guess I don't know that yet."

*An honest answer*, the angel said, *is always the right one. No other answer will get you where you want to go.*

"But I just said I don't...ohh."

In a flash, it all made sense. Jonah had *never* known where he wanted to go. He had never wanted to go any of the places he was *supposed* to want to go. He hadn't wanted to go to the big city, or to work in the small town. He still didn't know where he wanted to go.

But until now, he'd been assuming he was *supposed* to want to go where other people went. He'd assumed he was *supposed* to know where he was going, and that there must just have been something wrong with him if he didn't want what Mike Miller or his dad had.

Now that he was honest for the first time about the fact that he didn't *know* what he wanted, he could begin to figure it out.

*'Where do you want to go, Jonah?'*

He had no idea. But he knew he wanted to find out.

❉

Jonah moved slowly and carefully through the forest, stopping each time he thought he heard a sound. Around him, huge beasts crashed through the trees. Once or twice, he caught glimpses of blue-and-black mottled scaly hides or shaggy purple fur by the light of the glow vines. He was not afraid of them anymore. He had come this far: he was confident that he could reach his goal.

Every now and then, fairies flitted past him, giggling sweetly. He picked up his pace, then, eager to get away before they formed a swarm.

He listened most intently for another sound: the uneven, two-legged plodding of the old man, crashing through the underbrush. He was sure that his mentor would find him eventually - but was still a little anxious about leaving the old man with the fairies.

After what seemed like hours, Jonah began to doubt himself. Was he really sure he'd been traveling in a straight line, and not just in circles all this time? Would he ever find his way out of this darkness? He paused, considering turning back. The old man would know the way.

As he stood hesitating, a huge, monstrous *something* burst out of the trees to his right.It was headed straight toward him! Jonah dove to the ground with a yell, throwing his arms protectively over his head.

He lay on the ground, shaking, as the giant beast prowled around the clearing. He heard it growl low in its throat as it kneaded the leaves of the forest floor with huge paws, adorned with long, sharp close. He felt its huge nose nuzzle him. Its hot, damp breath smelled of rotting leaves. Jonah wished and prayed to be invisible.

"Excuse me," said a low, rough voice. "Are you alright?"

Jonah peered hesitantly up between his fingers, his eyes darting around the darkened clearing. He didn't see anyone who could have spoken.

The huge beast nudged him with its nose. "Excuse me?" the voice came again

Jonah turned his head slowly, disbelievingly, to look at the beast. It looked like a cross between a great, shaggy elephant and a giant aardvark. Its long sound was tipped with a soft nose, and it stared at him with huge, dark eyes.

"I...are you talking to me?" Jonah asked.

"Who else would I be talking to?" The beast's snout snuffled strangely as the voice issued from deep within its chest. Jonah blinked.

"Y-yeah. I'm fine. Thanks for asking."

The beast blinked and shoved its head closer to Jonah, staring at him intently with its huge eye. Jonah scrambled backward on the leaf litter, his heart pounding.

"I apologize if I scared you," the big beast snuffled slowly. "My eyesight isn't very good. I haven't seen a creature like you in my forest in quite some time. Are you lost?"

"Sort of," Jonah admitted. He hesitated. "Can you... help me?"

"Perhaps. What do you seek?"

"I'm supposed to - fight a dragon, I think. Something like that."

The huge, dark eye blinked in surprise. "A dragon? You? You're awfully small for that."

"I know," Jonah said. "I've got a mentor who said he'd teach me how. But I can't find him. Have you seen anybody else...like me?"

The beast made a long, loud snuffling sound that might

have been a laugh. "I think I know the one of whom you speak. No, I haven't seen him recently. But I can tell you where he always takes new adventurers, after this."

Jonah perked up. "Where?"

The great beast turned its head, pointing with its long nose off into the darkness. "There is a sea," it explained. "Its shore is about a days' journey from here. The dragon's lair is on an island just offshore. From there, the dragon rules the whole sea."

Jonah gulped, and tried not to think about fighting something that ruled an entire sea all by himself.

"You must cross a vast plain to get there. And if I recall - you can't eat after you leave this forest."

"I *what?*"

The beast made a terrifying movement of its massive shoulders. It took a moment for Jonah to register that as a shrug.

"I don't know why," the beast said slowly. "I was never much for adventuring and dragon-slaying. I prefer life here, with all these delicious fruits. But I always hear new adventurers complaining about that, when they're with the old man. He says they must 'fast to prepare their bodies and their minds,' or something. He makes them eat fruit before they leave, but won't let them take any with them."

Jonah bit his lip.

The huge animal glanced from one side of the clearing to another. It occurred to Jonah suddenly that the old beast was *bored* with the conversation, but was trying to be polite.

"Thank you very much for your help," he said quickly,

scrambling to his feet. "You're very kind - " Jonah started to say 'for a beast,' but it occurred to him that might be rude.

The great beast bowed, a majestic dip of its huge head. "Thank you. You have very good manners, for a human."

Then it plodded away through the trees, making a great crashing noise as it crushed underbrush beneath its paws.

# CHAPTER 8

Jonah walked in the direction the great beast had pointed, making his way slowly through the underbrush just like before. After a while, he found himself on a path that had clearly been traveled by others before. He wondered if those others had been human.

After following the path for a while, Jonah noticed that he could see some light filtering down from the tree tops. At first the light around him was dim, but it grew brighter, until he could see clear slivers of violet sky through the treetops.

Taking that as a sign that the forests' end was near, Jonah began keeping an eye out for copper-barked trees. Sure enough, he soon found a small copse of them growing along the side of the path. He set his intention, picturing a big, green fruit falling from the branches above. Then he knocked gently on the tree's trunk.

*Thud.* The big fruit plopped onto the forest floor, landing with a rustle in a nest of leaves. Jonah picked it up eagerly but cautiously, and decided to carry it to the edge of the forest before he ate.

With the big, green fruit under his arm, Jonah continued along the path, looking around in wonder as the forest thinned and a new, mysterious landscape emerged. There didn't seem to be any wall or gate on this side of the Garden - instead, it blended gradually into a grassland.

The grass that sprung up around Jonah's feet was the same vivid blue as the soft moss around the pool had been when Jonah first came to this world. Thinking about that day, he was amazed. His old life seemed a completely different reality now.

He knew that if - when- he went home, he would act completely differently, with a new sense of purpose and a new sense of power about his ability to change the world around him. Where before he had just accepted that things were the way they were and he was a child who had to follow the way things were, now he felt like he could see ways to make things better for everyone back in his old life. He almost felt a *duty* to make things better and more fulfilling for those around him.

He could help his mom try new hobbies, and some of the exotic foods she looked at in magazines. He could help his dad find time to read books, and go into the city sometimes to go to museums. Maybe he could start a club in town for people to think about how the world *could* be, instead of just how it had always been...

As Jonah got lost in thoughts of how he could use what he had learned here at home, he almost lost track of the grassland around him. So when he heard a voice say "Hello," he almost jumped out of his skin.

Jonah looked around anxiously for the source of the voice. Then, he felt relief flood him. It was the old man - sitting under a tree, which appeared to be the *last* tree he would encounter on his journey. Beyond that tree, flat, empty grassland spread to the horizon.

"I see you found your way out of the woods," the old man said cheerfully.

"I see you did too," Jonah said carefully, shifting the fruit into his lap as he sat down beside the old man.

"Oh yes. Fairies are annoying, but not dangerous. Not unless you fall for them." The old man peered at Jonah.

"Thanks for helping me get out of there," Jonah said sincerely. "Living just for pleasure might be right for some people - but it's not for me." Jonah held out his fruit. "I met a - creature - who said we would need this."

The old man smiled. "You spoke to a beast of the forest? Very impressive." He took the fruit, and began to carve it. "Did you remember to fill your water bottles?" he asked.

"I - shoot! I forgot!"

"It's not too late. There is a river near here. We'll follow it all the way to the sea - but you *will* want to fill those bottles every chance you get. The sea may be made of water, but you can't drink it."

"I've heard that you can't drink salt water," Jonah said, although he had a strange feeling the old man was talking about something else.

They ate the green fruit in contented silence, and it struck Jonah how *good* he felt. He'd been through terror and hardship, but that only made these simple pleasures all the sweeter - especially when he knew that what he was eating would strengthen him for the battle to come.

"The beast said," Jonah said, muffled, through a mouthful of fruit, "that I can't eat after this. Is that true?"

The old man nodded wisely. "Not for a day or so, anyway. There are a few reasons for this."

Jonah waited for the old man to explain.

"Did you know," the old man asked, swallowing a bite of fruit, "that it is healthy to fast for sixteen hours every now and then? During fasting your body switches to a healthier mode of metabolism, which can help you live longer, and strengthen your internal *organ*izational health."

The old man winked. "Internal organs. Get it?"

"You body heals in magical ways during fasting episodes. Food is not always the solution! In fact sometimes the body might need a short break from food."

*Live longer.* That got Jonah's attention. "How does that work?"

"No one is sure," the old man explained. "But as I've mentioned, our bodies are not really made to be surrounded by high-calorie foods all the time. Instead, they work best when they get only the nutrients they need, and not lots of extra calories.

""So...I only have to fast for sixteen hours, then? That sounds doable. I sleep for eight hours per night, anyway."

"Yes. But you *haven't* exactly been fasting while you've been in the fairy forest. So to get your metabolism right, I'm going to ask you to fast for a whole day."

Jonah squirmed uncomfortably.

"And there's another reason, too." Jonah waited.

"Very often, to get the things we want, we have to give up something we normally enjoy for a while. We do this because we can see the big picture - the final goal is fulfillment. To gain true fulfillment, we must often sacrifice pleasure.

"We may give up an expensive habit or hobby so we can do something even better with the money we save. We may give up a time-consuming habit or hobby so that we can use that time to do something great for ourselves. It is important to learn to make these trades, so that the great things we want are not kept out of our reach by the time and money costs of less important things.

"In this case, we are going to give up food for a day so that your metabolism can be in tip-top shape when we meet the dragon. You will find that your mind is clearer - as long as you make sure to drink plenty of water. Water is never a good thing to give up."

Jonah took a big bite of the green fruit slab in his hands. The old man peered at him.

"You don't have any blood sugar problems or medical conditions, do you Jonah? Each person's health is different, so some people need different approaches to good health."

"Not that I know of," Jonah said, thinking hard. "The town doctor never says anything about me having a health condition."

"Well then," the old man said, "let's get moving."

❈

The open plains were somehow even more mind-blowing than

the Desert of Doubt had been. In the Desert, the sand dunes had provided some texture to the landscape. Some of them had been so big that they reminded Jonah of the mountains and forests back home.

But here, the land was just *flat*. And that made it *feel* enormous. The blue grass and violet sky were particularly unsettling - Jonah had seen some grasslands back home, and seeing them stretch in every direction in the *wrong* color was - well, alien.

The old man, of course, was not bothered. He strode along a narrow path in the grass that had been cut by previous adventurers, whistling.

Jonah walked behind him, looking around uneasily. He had gotten used to the dark, dense forest hiding things from his sight. Now that he could see for miles around, some part of his mind felt that his eyes were lying to him.

After about an hours' walk, Jonah heard a *rushing* sound. The old man smiled happily and looked toward it.

Jonah saw it then - the Great River. He hadn't even noticed it until they were almost on top of it, because the land was so flat, and nothing grew out of it. But just a few meters away now was a giant groove in the grass. Within it, cerulean blue water rushed, gurgled, and splashed.

Remembering his ordeal in the Desert of Doubt, Jonah ran up to the river and knelt carefully by its bank. He tried not to think about what would happen if he slipped and fell in - he saw no roots or tree branches with which he could pull himself out. So he was very, very careful as he leaned out over the water with his uncapped, empty bottle and filled it to the brim.

When he raised the bottle to see if it was full, he was surprised to see that the water was *actually* blue. The color was not just a reflection of the grass and sky - his bottle looked as though it had been filled with blue paint!

"Is that…okay?" Jonah asked, glancing anxiously at the old man. The old man had stopped to fill his own bottles, whistling merrily as he did so.

"Oh yes. This isn't normal water, to be sure. But normal isn't always good. This water has - special properties."

Jonah's eyes widened. He wondered when the old man had been planning to tell him that.

"This water," the old man said mysteriously, "will change the way you see things. It will unlock things inside of you, and in the world around you, that have been hidden until now."

"That sounds…terrifying."

"It can be," the old man said. "But that's why it is good to take this journey with a friend. If anything happens that you can't handle - I will be here."

Jonah looked at the water in his bottle. If this was just the *lead up* to the dragon, he thought, then the dragon was going to be easy.

He filled all of his bottles and returned to pacing along behind the old man, sipping cautiously, a little at a time. The water tasted normal. If he had shut his eyes, he wouldn't have known there was anything different about it.

But as he walked, the world began to change.

First, he began to feel disoriented. It was as though the plains around him were moving, spinning. He squinted and kept his eyes on the old man, certain he knew where they were supposed to be going.

Then, suddenly, it seemed to Jonah as though he could see the ocean just ahead. He smelled salt air, and it seemed to him that he could feel the spray of sea foam on his face. He heard the waves crash against rocks - great waves and big, sharp rocks that separated him from a distant island.

On the island slept the largest living thing Jonah had ever seen.

He thought at first it was a strangely shaped castle, with big, sharp spires rising up into the sky. The sort of place you would expect to find a dragon. Then he realized that the spires were moving - the castle was *breathing*.

There was no castle at all. The castle *was* the dragon.

It was black in color, shiny, standing out sharply against the violet sky and blue sea. It appeared to be sleeping. As Jonah watched, it swished its tail in its sleep, kicking up huge waves as its tail cut the water and sent sea spray flying.

Jonah was trembling all over. He was afraid.

And then he was somewhere entirely different.

The dragon, the sound of the sea, and the smell of salt were gone. In their place, green meadows filled with sparkling flowers surrounded him on every side. Near the horizon, tall, proud pine trees like the ones in the mountains back home reached toward a blue sky.

*Jonah.*

By now, that sort of voice in his head was familiar to him. He looked toward where the angel stood in dazzling white radiance and watched its silhouette move gracefully.

*Why have you come here, Jonah?*

"Because I want to help people," he said bravely.

It felt strange to say that - he hadn't set out on this journey with that purpose in mind, but as he'd traveled, he had realized that's what it was. That was why being an auto mechanic didn't appeal to him, and neither did being a businessperson in the big city. He wanted to do something that resonated in his heart - even if it was hard, and sometimes felt impossible.

Now, he saw himself going back home, and changing his town for the better. He thought if he decided to go to the big city, he'd change that for the better, too. Maybe he could bring a little bit of the big city into his small town, and vice versa. Only the good things.

*Is that truly your answer?* The angel asked.

Jonah hesitated. It did feel like something someone might *want* him to say. He remembered what the old man had said about living for himself, and not caring what others thought.

But he didn't want to help people because he wanted them to like him or approve. In fact, the more he thought about it, the more he was sure that people around him would resist change at first - even if it was for the better.

His mother would wonder why he didn't just stay in his room anymore, and why he wanted to bring new things into the house. His father would wonder why Jonah wanted to try new things, and would wonder if he was getting "stuck up" like his dad said people in the city were.

But Jonah wanted to do it anyway, because he knew that it was good. He wanted to help people, and make the world a better place. Even if the people around him didn't always like that he was changing things.

"It is," he said firmly. He hoped that the angel might give him something to help him do that. As much as he was confident that he could start making changes, he wasn't yet sure that he could defeat the dragon, or create the better world he wanted back home.

*If that is what you want*, the angel said, *then you shall have it.*

The dark figure in the blinding light stretched out its hand. It was holding something. Jonah moved toward it, hesitantly. For some reason, he was sure the blinding light would burn.

But it didn't. As he moved into the blinding light, he felt nothing but profound peace, serenity, and joy. It was as though his mind grew quiet and he was aware of the joy of simply *being*.

His hand closed around the long, smooth shaft of a spear.

And for a moment, Jonah glimpsed something that knocked him backwards. For a moment the blinding light seemed to subside, and he could see the angel clearly in full color.

It was him.

The angel had his pale, pasty skin and freckles. It had his too-round face and red hair. He didn't see its clothes, but it wouldn't have surprised him at all of the angel were wearing his old, beat-up T-shirt and jeans.

Jonah fell back onto the grass, hard, and found himself looking up at the sky.

Above him, stars were visible, even though it was daylight. They shone brightly out of the heavens, as though radiating a divine message.

Below them, eagles circled - bald eagles, Jonah realized, with dark bodies and white heads.

*What...was that?*

Jonah didn't even know how to process what had happened. Had the angels been him all along? Then why hadn't he been able to hear their voices before coming to this place? Or was the universe trying to tell him something else - that he could *become* an angel?

Jonah had so many questions for the old man. But where *was* the old man?

Jonah sat up and looked around him. He looked down at the spear that was still clutched in his hand. Its point was long and sharp - terrifyingly so. It looked like something he'd seen in a movie about the Roman Empire, once.

He thought about slaying the dragon with this spear. He wondered what would happen when he did.

# CHAPTER 9

Suddenly, the world around Jonah seemed to flare. For an instant there was only blinding white radiance, like what surrounded the angels. Then, he was lying on his back, sprawled amidst long, blue grass. The sky above him was a deep violet, unnaturally bright stars peering out as the Sun sat on the horizon.

"Hello," the old man's voice came from nearby.

Jonah turned his head, and found that his body felt different from before. It felt stronger and lighter at once. It felt *clearer*, somehow.

He hefted the spear in his hand. And jumped.

"That was *real?*" Jonah exclaimed, backing away from the spear where it had fallen from his hand.

"It was as real as any experience is," the old man prodded him to approach the spear again. "And you're going to need that."

Jonah reached for it with trembling hands.

"Then, the dragon..."

"What did you see?"

"It was *huge*."

"Okay, yep," the old man confirmed. "Then that was real too."

Jonah looked at the old man and felt his mouth go dry.

The old man looked at him for a long, thoughtful minute. Behind him, the bright edge of the moon was beginning to peer over the horizon. "You know," the old man said gently, "you can still turn back if you want to. We can go home without facing the dragon, if it's - "

Jonah was surprised to find himself shaking his head violently. "No! I've come this far. I need to know that I can do this. If I can slay that dragon - I figure I can do anything. If not..." he trailed off.

"What happens," he asked finally, "if I try and fail?"

The old man shrugged. "That depends on the strength of the person.

"Some people are so scarred from failing to meet their goal that they are unhappy for the rest of their lives. They feel that the suffering they endured from the dragon's fire damaged them too badly to ever move past.

"But others pick themselves up and recover, and are happier for it. Some of them go back to their old lives, content that they have found their limits and learned a great deal in the process. Others come back and try again. Some people become *so* obsessed with slaying the dragon that they ignore everything else life has to offer - including the lessons offered by the journey. I don't recommend that."

This wasn't exactly making Jonah feel better. "Why are you

telling me this?" he asked, frightened, even though he knew he had *asked*.

"Because," the old man said, "you get to decide what kind of person you are. You get to decide whether you will feel so crushed by failure, and the hardship required for the journey, that you had better not even try. Or whether you will get so obsessed with the dragon that you forget your true purpose. Or whether you will learn from this journey - regardless of its outcome. How you respond is up to you. And it's better if I tell you of the dangers, so you can avoid them."

Jonah bit his lip. "So you're saying...you *don't* think I'll succeed?"

"I'm saying that it doesn't matter whether you succeed or not. When undertaking anything hard enough to be worth doing, you must be prepared to either fail *or* succeed. You must work for success with all your might, if the goal is really worth it - and if it's not, why are you bothering?

"But you must also recognize that not all the factors are within your control. Maybe there will be a storm, and you will slip off the dragon's island and into the sea. Maybe the dragon will be feeling particularly peppy that day, and he'll burn you to a crisp. Maybe you will slay him, and find out what comes next.

"You have to be prepared for every outcome, and accept the potential costs against the potential benefits. That's why I'm saying we can still turn around."

"No," Jonah decided. "I think - I think I understand the costs and benefits. I would rather try than live my life knowing I didn't even try."

The old man's face split into an enormous grin. "That's a

good lad!" He sat down on the ground next to Jonah. "Now, we'd better get some rest. If all goes well, we'll reach the sea by midday tomorrow."

Jonah rolled over on the grass, and tried not to think about what might not 'go well.'

❄

Jonah woke at dawn the next day, excitement coursing through him. He was surprised by his own response. He should have been terrified, but instead he felt pure focus and determination.

He shook the old man roughly to wake him, took both of their empty bottles and scampered down to the river to refill him. Halfway down the bank, he realized that his body felt *strange*.

He was moving differently from how he normally moved. He almost felt like his muscles and bones were working together in a new way. He held his head high with confidence, his shoulders back and his chest broad as he felt about the angel and the spear.

In his mind's eye, the angel had started to look like a Roman gladiator - strong, confident, powerful. That was how angels should look, Jonah thought. Like people who knew right from wrong, and were ready to do something about it. He imagined exercising, going to the gym and to yoga classes until he stood straight and confident, and trusted the strength of his arms and legs.

Back home, he'd always hated going to the gym - and especially yoga classes, because he was so bad at them. He didn't like reminding people of his soft, pasty body or how awkward he felt when he moved. He didn't like practicing things he was sure he'd never be good at, or things that made him sore the next day.

But now, he felt he *could* do those things. He could learn to lift weights if he tried hard. He could learn to do those crazy yoga poses that the girls could do, but that he found quickly exhausting and frustrating. He could reshape his body if he wanted to. It couldn't possibly hurt more, or be scarier, than passing through the Desert of Doubt.

Jonah looked at his reflection in the river and was surprised to see that he *already* looked like what he imagined. The person in his reflection had his face, for sure - his bone structure, his freckles, his sharp green eyes.

But on that face, they looked somehow charming, daring - even *dashing*, he thought, the way his mom described the lead actors in old movies.

Nothing about his bone structure or coloring had changed - but he now realized that every muscle and curve of his body reflected his attitude and emotions. Now that those had changed completely, his posture and expression and the way he moved had changed, too.

He was still Jonah - but he was a completely *new* Jonah who was better than he'd ever thought that he could be.

Jonah strode confidently back up the bank, his arms loaded with bottles of blue water. He slipped them into his bag and the old man's bag as the old man rubbed his eyes blearily.

"At this rate," the old man said, "you're going to be moving faster than me."

Jonah only smiled.

He led the way this time as they struck out across the blue plains, toward the sea.

# CHAPTER 10

It was midday when the sea came into sight.

At first, it was visible only as a change to the color of the horizon. The sea was a dark, deeper blue than the grass, partially reflecting the color of the sky.

Even from that great distance, the dragon's island was visible: a black spot against the line of blue that was the sea.

As they grew nearer, Jonah's heart began to pound.

"So, I might get burned, right?" he asked the old man. He wanted to make sure he was clear on what might happen.

"That is correct," the old man confirmed. "You may be burned a little, or quite badly."

"And if I'm burned badly...?"

"It will hurt. But it won't kill you."

"That's...good to know."

Jonah tried to imagine how he would attack the dragon. Part of him almost didn't want to ask for help, wanted to figure this out on his own. But, he thought - what if he failed because there was some trick or technique he did not know?

"How would you...attack the dragon, if you were going to do it?" Jonah asked, as the dragon grew larger in his view. From here, he could see its tail swishing sleepily over the water.

The old man regarded him sidelong. "I'd go for the eyes. That's the only way to do it, really. It's the only place the dragon isn't armored. But to get there..."

"I'll have to climb up its neck, close to its mouth," Jonah finished. His own mouth went dry.

He remembered how scared he had felt as he lay on the ground, praying that the beast in the Garden wouldn't eat him. Knowing he was no match for its size, for the length of its claws.

He tried to imagine feeling more scared than that.

"Do you know what the secret to this is, Jonah?" the old man asked.

"Other than 'go for the eyes?'"

"The secret is to face your fear. To make *friends* with your fear. Do you know why?"

"That sounds insane," Jonah said flatly.

"It's because everything you want is on the other side of fear."

Those words resonated through Jonah's body, and his eyes widened.

Just like that, he was back in his body - his *old* body, back home.

He wanted to ask out Chrissy Thomas to the dance, but

he was too scared to even talk to her. He was afraid she would reject him.

He fantasized about being on the football team, but he was too scared to try out. Surely, he would be the weakest person there. He was afraid that people would make fun of him.

He thought about applying to that prestigious college out west, but why bother? He was afraid they would reject him, too, and it would just have been a waste of time.

And yet, now he thought about it from the other side.

What might he have *gained* if he had asked Chrissy out? She might have rejected him, sure, but now that he had seen this strong, confident version of himself, he knew that she might *not* have rejected him. What was the risk of rejection compared to what he would have gained if she'd said "yes?"

What might he have *gained* if he had tried out for the football team, not caring what anyone else thought? What if he had gone to the gym, not caring if anyone teased him? What was the risk of teasing compared to having a strong, healthy body?

What might he have *gained* if he had applied to that school? Sure, they might have rejected him. But the time he spent on the application would be nothing compared to the benefits if he got in.

"Everything you want," the old man repeated, "is on the other side of fear. In fact, fear can be a helpful guidepost to tell you where to go. If you move in the direction of your fear, if you move toward doing *more* of what you are afraid of, your abilities and power will grow faster than you could possibly imagine. Every time you do something you are afraid of, you gain a new ability that you did not have before."

Jonah blinked in awe of how true that was. How many things had he not done in his life because of fear? How many things had he assumed would never be possible for him because they scared him?

What if he used fear to tell him what he *should* do, instead of what he shouldn't? What if he had done all the things he was afraid of?

He would be a completely different person, Jonah realized. He would be the same Jonah - with the same desires, feelings, likes, and dislikes. But he would be able to do whatever he wanted, without fear. If he didn't have a skill he needed to do something he wanted, he'd simply build it, because he would have no fear of embarrassment or failure.

He wondered what he'd be doing instead of hiding in his room reading comic books all these years, if he had always acted that way.

They were at the shoreline now, where red-gold sand was lapped by dark blue waves. A few hundred feet offshore, the dragon slumbered like a mountain, its scales shining sully in the evening light.

"And that," the old man finished, "is why you're here. If you can face this dragon, you can defeat any fear. Then there will be nothing in the world you can't do."

Jonah took a deep breath. He felt the sea spray on this face and smelled the salt on the air.

"So," he said, "I guess I walk alone from here, huh?"

❄

The water was cold and sharp against his skin. It cut into him like knives as he swam, spear in hand.

The waves grew taller and more powerful as he approached the dragon's island. The great splashes of its tail hit him, sometimes picking him up and throwing him into the air, or crashing over his head and submerging him meters underwater.

Jonah spit the salt out of his mouth, and kept swimming. Just when he was sure that he was too exhausted, that he was going to drown before he even reached the island, his foot touched a sharp rock. He flailed in the direction of the rock, and soon his other foot touched another. And another.

Within a few minutes, he was walking on solid ground. Gasping and dripping, Jonah waded out of the water, using the shaft of his spear like a third leg to balance him when he slipped on the wet rocks.

He looked up at the dragon that towered over him like a mountain, dark and ominous. He could see its sides heaving with breath more powerful than he could imagine. Here he was, out of breath - and the dragon hadn't even bothered to stir from its slumber yet.

Jonah approached one of the dragon's scaly front feet. As he walked, he realized he was not shaking just from cold. He was terrified. What would happen if he failed?

*What would happen if he succeeded?*

*Move in the direction of your fear.*

On trembling legs, he stepped up to the dragon's foot and laid his hands on it. It was smooth and warm. He flinched, half-expecting the dragon to rear its head and roar. But the dragon hadn't even noticed him yet. To it, he was only a gnat.

Jonah began to climb.

It was difficult going, the smooth scales under his wet feet. But at least the dragon's warmth warmed Jonah too, and as he climbed up from the feet, the scales became rougher and craggier, easier to keep his footing on.

When Jonah had gotten to the dragon's elbow, the dragon stirred. The whole world seemed to move and shake. Jonah clutched the scales under him, terrified. His knuckles were white around the shaft of his spear.

The spear was beginning to seem quite pitiful a weapon against such a monster.

The ground under him *shifted*. The directions of "up" and "down" moved with it. Jonah was raised high in the air, the sea and the island dropping away beneath him as the dragon stretched its front legs. He hung on for dear life.

At least while the dragon stretched, its arm was almost horizontal. Jonah took the advantage to scramble further along the craggy surface of the dragon's scales, toward its shoulder.

The dragon stopped moving. It froze, its arm in midair.

Scorching hot breath seared Jonah's back.

Above him, a giant, slit-pupiled eye stared down at him.

For a moment, Jonah and the dragon only looked at each other. Then, Jonah jumped.

He made the jump between the dragon's shoulder and its neck frantically, knowing he would not get another chance. Sure enough, the dragon began to thrash violently, trying to shake him off. Jonah had to stop and simply hang on for a few moments, as the beast under him tossed from side-to-side.

Fear began to get the better of him again. He was sweating. He had never been so afraid. While he was moving, he could concentrate on that. But now that he was still, he asked himself:

*What the heck am I doing here?*

He was Jonah the nerd, not Jonah the dragon slayer. Anyone else should be here - anyone but him. He should be at home, under his covers, reading about Batman.

Jonah ignored the voice of Doubt, and moved on.

Having failed to throw him off by flailing, the dragon stopped thrashing and lifted one enormous paw. The movement was so slow and profound, it was like the Earth was moving.

Jonah reached the spines on the dragon's neck, and used them to pull himself forward, as the climb grew steeper, and drop onto the rocks below grew ever-longer.

The dragon tried to claw him off. Razor-sharp claws the size of his house raked across the dragon's neck. One of them missed him by only inches. He clung to one of the dragon's spines and tried to use it as a shield, blocking the sharp claws from reaching them.

He had nearly reached the head, by now.

The hardest part, he knew, was yet to come. The dragon would be able to thrash its head wildly, and would surely throw him off. For a moment, he could see no way to get to the eye, to cover the remaining distance, without being thrown to his death.

And then he saw that there was only one way.

Jonah lunged forward and grabbed the small, sharp spine that rose from the back of the dragon's neck. He hung onto it for dear life, as the dragon began to toss its head this way and that, violently throwing Jonah around like a rag doll. There was no way he could let go of the spine to climb to the dragon's eye, now.

There was no way he could *climb* there.

Jonah waited, clinging, until he had a feel for the dragon's movements. He watched its eye, trying to memorize its location in relation to himself.

Beneath him, the dragon began to raise its head vigorously, moving to throw Jonah straight up into the air. Jonah took a deep breath - and let go.

He felt the dragon fall away beneath him. He flailed through the air, out of control, and for a moment he was sure he was going to die.

Time seemed to slow down. The dragon's huge mouth with its sharp teeth was opening. Within the darkness of its throat, a glow like embers rose from its belly. It was preparing to breathe fire, and burn him to a crisp in midair.

Jonah plummeted downward - and directly into the dragon's mouth.

Head. Searing heat, all over his body. It was worse than anything he'd felt before - worse than when he'd burned his hand on the stove, or grabbed that friction-hot tool in auto shop.

But he didn't give up. As he plummeted, he clutched his spear in both hands and threw all his weight behind it. Around him, the flesh of the dragon's throat was soft and vulnerable.

All of his brain's barriers, fears and doubt evaporated in

the heat of the dragon's throat. He thrust the spear into the dragon's throat, and darkness closed in around him -

*Splash.*

*Water.*

Jonah emerged, spluttering and gasping, to find himself surrounded by tall pine trees. The air smelled different. It smelled like -

*Home.*

He got to his feet and staggered out of the forest pool, moving without thinking. He stumbled back onto the dry leaf litter, and realized that pale, early morning sun was filtering through the trees all around him.

The old man stood a few feet away from Jonah, leaning on a walking stick. He winked at him. Only then did Jonah notice what he was holding in his own hand - in place of a spear, it was a walking stick just like the old man's.

"What - happened?" Jonah gasped. He hadn't thought much about what would happen after he slayed the dragon - but he hadn't expected *this*. Part of him at least wanted to see its majestic carcass lying vanquished on the island, while the people of the land cheered -

But people cheering him on wasn't really the point, was it?

"You passed the test," the old man said simply. "You reached the end - of that journey." Then, the old man made a sweeping gesture - encompassing the forest, the nearby town, the mountains and parks, and the big cities in the far distance.

"But this world," he said, "has many more journeys to offer." Jonah turned to look at the trees, the distant twinkling lights of the town.

He turned back, his mouth open to answer the old man.

But the old man was gone.

Jonah wanted to thank the old man for all he had done. For the first time, Jonah had clarity and purpose. He knew that with the vision and courage he'd gained, his life would become magnificent!

But he also thought he knew why the old man had disappeared.

If Jonah couldn't thank the one who taught him, he'd have to pay it forward.

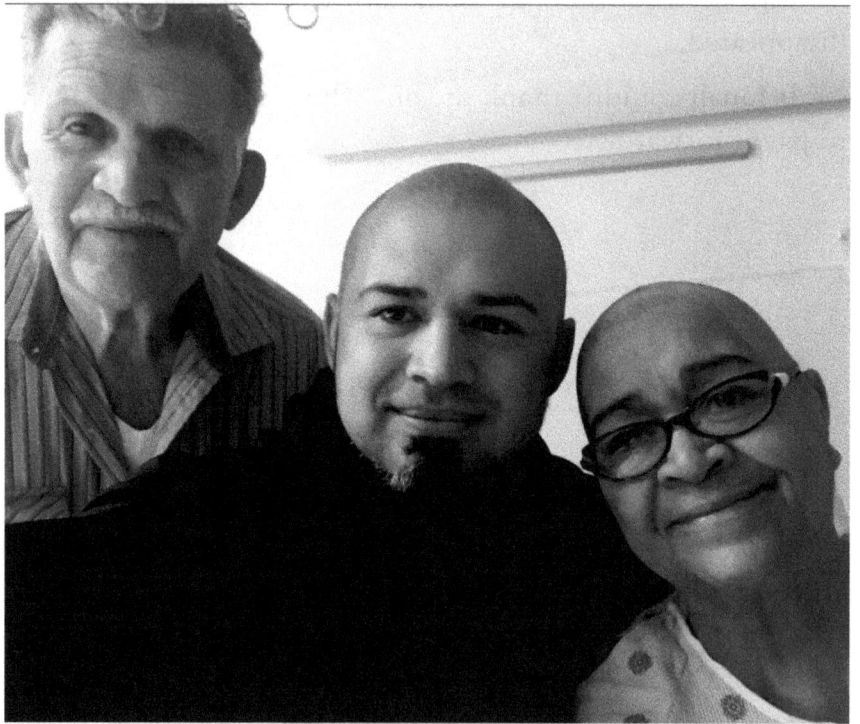

# About The Author

Carlos Kano grew up in a small town in California. He uses modern myths to take his readers on a hero's journey, from the ordinary world of everyday life into the mystical realm of the possible.

He dedicates this book to anyone who knows, deep down in their heart, that they are not living their best life. He hopes this story will provide the inspiration to support you in getting started.

www.ingramcontent.com/pod-product-compliance
Lightning Source LLC
Chambersburg PA
CBHW072043040426
42447CB00012BB/3000